THE CLEAR AND PRESENT TRUTH OF THE
ABOMINATION OF DESOLATION

Rapid Movements Publishing
Hampton, GA 30228

Copyright © 2021 by Tory St.Cyr

Printed in the United States of America

All Rights Reserved

Published by Rapid Movements Publishing
Hampton, GA 30228

Other books by Tory St.Cyr may be purchased at
www.clearandpresenttruth.com

The author assumes full responsibility for the accuracy of all facts and quotations, as cited in this book.

ISBN: 978-1-7366073-1-2

Internal pictures and illustrations used by permission of creative commons license:

By © José Luiz Bernardes Ribeiro, CC BY-SA 4.0,
https://commons.wikimedia.org/w/index.php?curid=62549846

By François-Louis Dejuinne - http://fr.academic.ru/dic.nsf/frwiki/180423,
Public Domain,
https://commons.wikimedia.org/w/index.php?curid=3710441

This book is written in remembrance
of the millions of individuals who have been affected
by the Abomination of Desolation.

Contents

Preface 9
The Event 11
Whoso Readeth, Let Him Understand 23
A Second Abomination of Desolation 33
    Antiochus Epiphanes 33
    Clovis I 42
    The Bishop of Rome 51
A Third Abomination of Desolation 59
TEST YOUR KNOWLEDGE 71
ANSWERS 74

Preface

The Abomination of Desolation is a topic that has always interested me. However, I never dedicated much study time to this subject because I assumed I understood it. It wasn't until I began doing research for this book that I discovered there is more to the Abomination of Desolation than I initially thought.

Many have defined the Abomination of Desolation as something terrible or very sinful. This broad definition often leads some of us to simply look for a terrible or sinful occurrence and designate it as the Abomination of Desolation. However, the Bible reveals a specific event that is defined as the Abomination of Desolation. This definition should be consistent anywhere the Abomination of Desolation is found in scripture. The reason many are misinterpreting the Abomination of Desolation is that they are deviating from this definition. In this book, you will be given the Biblical meaning of the Abomination of Desolation, and you will understand how this phrase is still relevant today.

The Daily Sacrifice and the Abomination of Desolation are closely affiliated with each other as seen in Daniel 11:31 and Daniel 12:11. Therefore, before you read this book, I suggest you read this book's predecessor, *The Clear and Present Truth of the Daily Sacrifice.*

By the time you finish these two books, I genuinely believe you will have a brand-new outlook on prophecy.

Chapter 1

The Event

Jesus intently looked at His disciples as he declared the events that would occur in Jerusalem after His death. The disciples listened as Jesus spoke about the false Christ's that would come upon the world. They heard Jesus declare that nations and kingdoms would be involved in wars and rumors of wars. They understood that one day famines would plague the earth, diseases would become more prevalent, and earthquakes would increase. The disciples heard everything Jesus declared would fall upon Jerusalem, yet they did not fully understand.

The prophecy given in the 24th chapter of Matthew was two-fold. Jesus had not only revealed the terrors of the last days, He also warned them of the soon-coming destruction of Jerusalem. Had the disciples fully understood that Jesus would be crucified and Jerusalem would be destroyed soon afterward, they would've been overwhelmed with horror. It was God's mercy to veil the future from the disciples at that time;

however, their understanding would increase as events would unfold.[1] Jesus continued his discourse but focused on the immediate fate of the glorious city. He looked at his disciples and made this solemn declaration:

> "When ye therefore shall see the abomination of desolation, spoken of by Daniel the prophet, stand in the holy place, (whoso readeth, let him understand:) Then let them which be in Judaea flee into the mountains: Let him which is on the housetop not come down to take any thing out of his house: Neither let him which is in the field return back to take his clothes. And woe unto them that are with child, and to them that give suck in those days! But pray ye that your flight be not in the winter, neither on the sabbath day." Matthew 24:15-20

The urgency in Christ's tone was an indication that a small window would be afforded to those who wished to escape the coming onslaught. However, Jesus made sure His disciples understood there would be an event that would act as a trigger for this departure from

---

[1] Ellen White, The Great Controversy (Mountain View, CA: Pacific Press Publishing Association, 1911) p. 25

Jerusalem. He declared, "*When ye therefore shall see the abomination of desolation, spoken of by Daniel the prophet, stand in the holy place. Then let them which be in Judaea flee into the mountains.*" According to Jesus, the Abomination of Desolation was the event that would act as an alarm for the believers to flee Jerusalem.

Today, the meaning of the Abomination of Desolation continues to be the subject of many disputes; however, every Christian that lived during the destruction of Jerusalem understood exactly what Christ meant. Think about it from this perspective: What sense would it make for Jesus to warn believers about the destruction of Jerusalem, but the believers misunderstand how to avoid that destruction? It's possible that the believers misunderstood Him at that moment, but when the Abomination of Desolation showed up, they recognized the sign and fled Jerusalem before it was destroyed.

I was curious to know for myself what did Jesus mean when He said, "*Abomination of Desolation.*" I decided that in order to understand its meaning, I needed to define both *Abomination* and *Desolation* separately. I assumed that once I broke the phrase down into its simplest form, I would easily be able to grasp the meaning behind Jesus' words to His followers. I found an online Lexicon (vocabulary dictionary) and looked up the word *Abomination*. Here is what was written:

> Abomination: a detestation, i.e. (specially) idolatry: —abomination.[2]

Strong's definition of abomination was precisely what I thought it would be—something horrible. However, this definition was so broad that almost any sin could be considered an abomination to the Lord. On the other hand, when Jesus said, "*The Abomination of Desolation*," I felt He was being very specific, so specific that this particular Abomination resulted in something called Desolation.

I decided to look up the word Desolation in that same Lexicon. If Abomination could not help shed light on the meaning of Christ's words, then I truly believed the meaning of Desolation would. The Greek Lexicon defines Desolation as follows:

> Desolation: to lay waste (literally or figuratively): —(bring to, make) desolate(-ion), come to nought.[3]

According to this definition, desolation emphasizes the *results* of destruction over the *act* of destroying. In other words, the desolation of Jerusalem hadn't yet occurred when the Romans broke down the

---

[2] "G946 - bdelygma - Strong's Greek Lexicon (KJV)." Blue Letter Bible. Accessed 17 Sep, 2020.
https://www.blueletterbible.org//lang/lexicon/lexicon.cfm?Strongs=G946&t=KJV
[3] "G2049 - erēmoō - Strong's Greek Lexicon (KJV)." Blue Letter Bible. Accessed 17 Sep, 2020.
https://www.blueletterbible.org//lang/lexicon/lexicon.cfm?Strongs=G2049&t=KJV

walls of the holy city. Likewise, the desolation had not taken place, even as the Romans began slaughtering the Jewish citizens. And even when the Romans battered the Jewish temple, the desolation still had not taken place. It wasn't until the onslaught ended, and lifeless bodies lay scattered all over the streets, and one stone could not be found upon another, that the desolation was evident.

Now that I understood the meaning of abomination and the meaning of desolation, I concluded that the Abomination of Desolation was something evil that resulted in ruin. This definition made sense to me, but it didn't get me closer to understanding the specific Abomination that led to the specific Desolation referred to by Jesus.

At this point, I decided to see if any of the other Gospels recorded this same conversation between Christ and His disciples. Even though the Gospels are part of the same Bible, they express four distinct perspectives of Christ's life; therefore, if you are unclear on one Gospel's perspective, another Gospel may provide a clearer context. I discovered Luke recorded this same conversation; however, there's a clear difference in Luke's portrayal of the exchange between Jesus and His disciples than what was recorded in Matthew. Luke recorded the words of Christ as follows:

> "And when ye shall see Jerusalem compassed with armies, then know that the desolation thereof is nigh. Then let them which are in Judaea flee to the mountains; and let them which are in the midst of it depart out; and let not them that are in the countries enter thereinto." Luke 21:20-21

There it is! The Gospel of Luke didn't leave me to my own imagination to determine what the Abomination of Desolation was. He made it clear that the event Matthew recorded as the Abomination of Desolation would be fulfilled when Jerusalem would be compassed or surrounded with armies. These surrounding armies would later result in the complete destruction of Jerusalem. Notice how Ellen White expresses these same sentiments:

> "When the idolatrous standards of the Romans should be set up in the holy ground, which extended some furlongs outside the city walls, then the followers of Christ were to find safety in flight. When the warning sign should be seen, those who would escape must make no delay. Throughout the land of Judea, as well

as in Jerusalem itself, the signal for flight must be immediately obeyed. He who chanced to be upon the housetop must not go down into his house, even to save his most valued treasures. Those who were working in the fields or vineyards must not take time to return for the outer garment laid aside while they should be toiling in the heat of the day. They must not hesitate a moment, lest they be involved in the general destruction." *The Great Controversy* p. 26

I hope we have clearly established that the Abomination of Desolation was not when the Romans breached the walls of Jerusalem. At that time, it would've been too late for any of the Christians to escape the onslaught, which would've made Christ's warning pointless. Understand, the Abomination of Desolation was when the Roman armies *surrounded* Jerusalem, which later led to its destruction.

In simplified terms, the surrounding of Jerusalem by the Pagan-Roman army was the Abomination. The results of the city walls being breached and the onslaught that ensued was the Desolation.

History tells us that Jerusalem was destroyed in 70 AD by the Roman General, Titus.[4] However, in the book, *The Great Controversy*, we are told that not one Christian perished with the city.

> "Not one Christian perished in the destruction of Jerusalem. Christ had given His disciples warning, and all who believed His words watched for the promised sign. "When ye shall see Jerusalem compassed with armies," said Jesus, "then know that the desolation thereof is nigh. Then let them which are in Judea flee to the mountains; and let them which are in the midst of it depart out." Luke 21:20, 21. After the Romans under Cestius had surrounded the city, they unexpectedly abandoned the siege when everything seemed favorable for an immediate attack. The besieged, despairing of successful resistance, were on the point of surrender, when the Roman general withdrew his forces without the least apparent reason. But God's merciful

---

[4] Encyclopædia Britannica, s.v. " Siege of Jerusalem," last modified August 29, 2018, https://www.britannica.com/event/Siege-of-Jerusalem-70

providence was directing events for the good of His own people. The promised sign had been given to the waiting Christians, and now an opportunity was offered for all who would, to obey the Saviour's warning. Events were so overruled that neither Jews nor Romans should hinder the flight of the Christians. Upon the retreat of Cestius, the Jews, sallying from Jerusalem, pursued after his retiring army; and while both forces were thus fully engaged, the Christians had an opportunity to leave the city. At this time the country also had been cleared of enemies who might have endeavored to intercept them. At the time of the siege, the Jews were assembled at Jerusalem to keep the Feast of Tabernacles, and thus the Christians throughout the land were able to make their escape unmolested. Without delay they fled to a place of safety—the city of Pella, in the land of Perea, beyond Jordan."
The Great Controversy, p. 30-31

At this point, it was clear to me that when these Roman soldiers surrounded Jerusalem, it was essentially a Pagan nation on the grounds of what was considered a holy city. This is why Matthew wrote, "*The Abomination of Desolation...stand*[ing] *in the holy place.*" Mark recorded this same conversation, but instead of using the phrase "*holy place,*" he says, "*But when ye shall see the abomination of desolation...standing where it ought not...*" Both Matthew's "*holy place,*" and *Mark's "where it ought not,"* make the same point—That when the Roman armies ventured onto the grounds of Jerusalem with all their idolatry and Pagan superstition, it was an Abomination! This invasion of Paganism onto God's holy ground tells us the true definition of the Abomination of Desolation. The Abomination of Desolation occurs when God's territory is invaded by Satanic forces, which eventually brings ruin to God's people.

Now that we have properly defined the Abomination of Desolation, I need you to understand that this definition will never change. This definition is, and will always be, the occupation of God's territory by Satanic forces. It is vital that you understand this point because the remainder of this book hinges on it.

At this point, I'm sure someone reading this chapter is wondering how there can be additional chapters to this book when we've already uncovered the true meaning of the Abomination of Desolation. What else is there to understand? Technically, we could end the book here and enter it into the Guinness World

THE EVENT • 21

Records for the shortest book ever published. However, we cannot end the book here because there is more to the Abomination of Desolation—more than you may realize. Remember, Jesus said, "*Whoso readeth, let him understand.*" The questions we need to answer are—What is being read? And what needs to be understood?

Chapter 2

Whoso Readeth, Let Him Understand

We've established what the Abomination of Desolation is. However, what hasn't been established is what Jesus meant, in Matthew 24:15, when He said, "*Whoso readeth, let him understand.*" The first question we need to answer is — Whoso readeth *what*?

I found the answer to this question in the same verse where Jesus, referring to the Abomination of Desolation, says, "*...spoken of by Daniel the prophet.*" Here, Jesus gives us a clear indication that the Abomination of Desolation was initially prophesied by Daniel. So when Jesus said, "*Whoso readeth,*" the context was the reading of the prophecies found in the Book of Daniel.

So now that we've established what is being read, we must determine what Jesus meant when he said, "*Let him understand.*" In order for us to understand what needed to be understood, we must refer back to the Book of Daniel and notate all the references made to the Abomination of Desolation. I discovered three verses that contained the word "abomination" or "desolation." Here they are:

> "Then I heard one saint speaking, and another saint said unto that certain saint which spake, How long shall be the vision concerning the daily sacrifice, and the transgression[5] of desolation, to give both the sanctuary and the host to be trodden under foot?" Daniel 8:13

> "And arms shall stand on his part, and they shall pollute the sanctuary of strength, and shall take away the daily sacrifice, and they shall place the abomination that maketh desolate." Daniel 11:31

> "And from the time that the daily sacrifice shall be taken away, and the abomination that maketh desolate set up, there shall be a thousand two

---

[5] In Daniel 8:13, the word transgression is used instead of abomination. The term is different, but the context of the transgression and the abomination appear to refer to the same event.

hundred and ninety days." Daniel 12:11

Here, Daniel made three references to the Abomination of Desolation. When I initially read these scriptures, I assumed this is what Jesus was referring to when He warned his disciples about the destruction of Jerusalem. I also noticed these three scriptures mentioned a Daily Sacrifice being taken away. Since I was under the impression these references to the Abomination of Desolation referred to the destruction of Jerusalem, I also concluded that the taking away of the Daily Sacrifice referred to the Crucifixion of Christ. However, I soon began to see that this view was problematic. After further research, I realized the only way to conclude these scriptures were talking about the Crucifixion of Christ and the destruction of Jerusalem was to rewrite history itself! I know these are strong words but let me show you why they are applicable in this situation.

Take another look at Daniel 12:11. This verse says, "*from the time that the daily sacrifice shall be taken away and the abomination that maketh desolate set up, there shall be 1290 days.*" According to my calculation, 1290 days is equivalent to 43 months or three years and seven months.[6] Now we need to determine if this timeframe correlates in any way to the Crucifixion and

---

[6] Each month is composed of 30 days.

the destruction of Jerusalem. If the 1290-day period aligns with these two events, then Jesus declaring "*whoso readeth let him understand*" was simply Christ's method of emphasizing Jerusalem's future desolation, and there is no further understanding to be acquired. However, if we determine that the 1290-day period has no relation to the Crucifixion and the Abomination of Desolation, then this is an indication that Jesus was referring to another Abomination of Desolation—one which I overlooked.

In order to make this determination, let's take a look at three ways to chart the 1290 days and how they might correlate to the Crucifixion and the destruction of Jerusalem.

First view:
1290 days occur *between* the Daily Sacrifice being taken away and the Abomination of Desolation being set up.

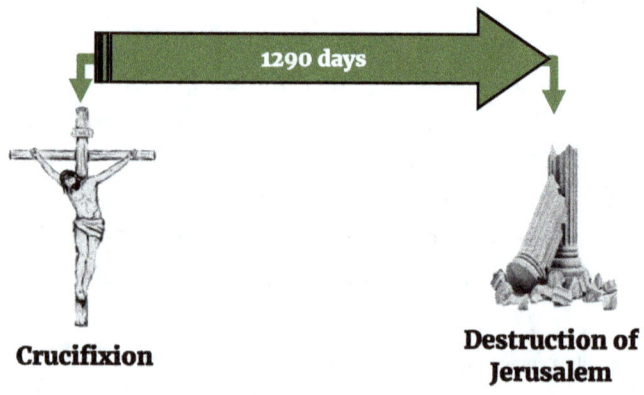

Crucifixion　　　　　　　　**Destruction of Jerusalem**

Let's look at this first view, which promotes the idea of a 1290-day layover between the Daily Sacrifice being taken away and the Abomination of Desolation being set up. Assuming the prophecy is describing Christ's Crucifixion, and the destruction of Jerusalem poses an obvious issue. The issue is Christ was crucified in 31 AD[7], and Jerusalem was destroyed in 70 AD—nearly 40 years later. This eliminates the idea of a 1290-*day* time span between these two events; however, we must also be open to the possibility that the 1290 days are not literal.

According to Numbers 14:34, there is a principle in Bible prophecy that determines a day equals a year when the fulfillment of that prophecy is contingent on a time span. Applying the day-for-a-year principle to this prophecy declares a 1290-*year* time span between the taking away of the Daily Sacrifice and the setting-up of the Abomination of Desolation. Unfortunately, this view presents an equally problematic theory. If Jerusalem were destroyed 1290 years after the Crucifixion, this would mean history was wrong, and Jerusalem was not destroyed in 70 AD but remained intact until 1321 AD. I don't think we need to detail the obvious issues caused by embracing this theory. This would result in a domino effect and force us to call into question almost every world event known to humanity.

---

[7] Colin J. Humphreys and W. G. Waddington, "Dating the Crucifixion," Nature 306 (December 22/29, 1983), pp. 743-46

So before I cause a historical apocalypse, let me declare right now, there wasn't a 1290-year gap between the Crucifixion of Christ and the destruction of Jerusalem (Disaster averted).

It was clear to me, whether I viewed the 1290 days literally or prophetically, this timeframe did not occur between the Crucifixion and the destruction of Jerusalem.

Jesus said, "*Whoso readeth let him understand*." I was reading, but I clearly didn't understand what Jesus meant.

Second view:
The taking away of the Daily Sacrifice and the setting up of the Abomination of Desolation both occur at the *end* of 1290 days.

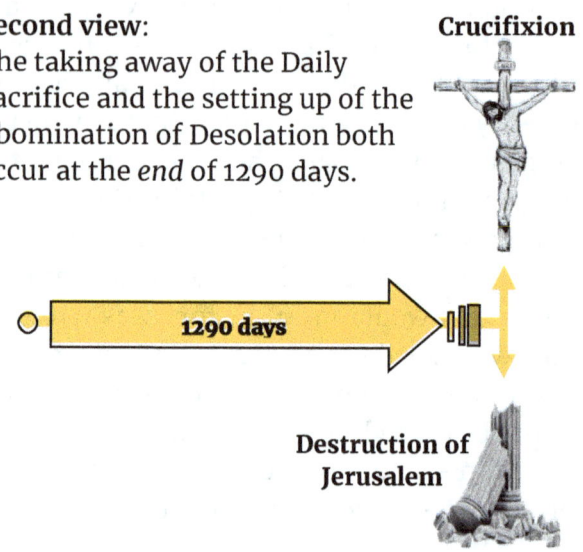

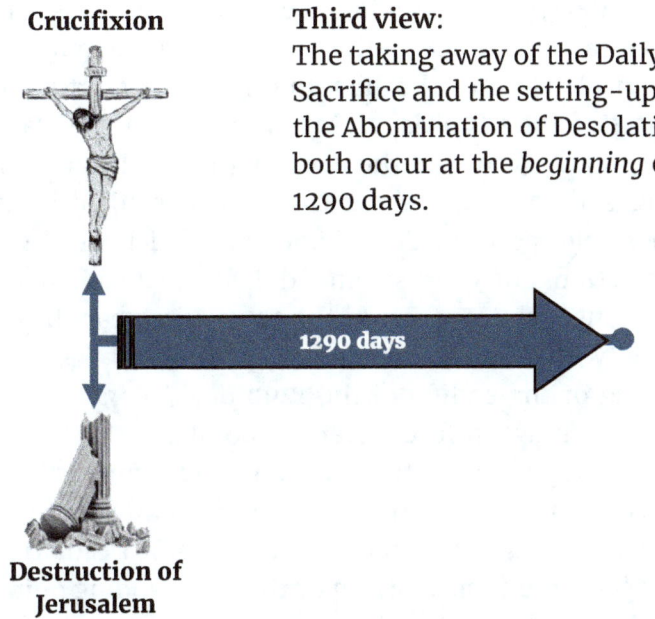

Third view:
The taking away of the Daily Sacrifice and the setting-up of the Abomination of Desolation both occur at the *beginning* of 1290 days.

Now, let's look at the second and third views. Both theories embrace the idea that the Daily Sacrifice being taken away and the Abomination of Desolation being set up were the starting or ending points of the 1290 days/years. Let's again assume the taking away of the Daily Sacrifice represented Christ's Crucifixion, and this setting-up of the Abomination of Desolation represented the destruction of Jerusalem. Essentially, Daniel would be telling us that "From the time the Crucifixion takes place, and the destruction of Jerusalem occurs, there will be 1290 days/years" (or

1290 days/years would have already passed). Understand, embracing either position creates another historical dilemma; the dilemma is that the starting or ending of the 1290 days/years relies upon the Daily being taken away *and* the Abomination of Desolation being set up at the same time. This is historically impossible as the Crucifixion of Christ and the destruction of Jerusalem did not take place simultaneously. How could the 1290 days/years begin or end with both events? It is impossible to base the starting or the ending of the 1290 days/years off two events with two different starting points.

Simply put, the second and third views determine that the taking away of the Daily Sacrifice and the setting-up of the Abomination of Desolation must have the same starting or the same ending point. The fact that the Crucifixion and the destruction of Jerusalem were forty years apart reveals that either Daniel was mistaken, or Jesus was referring to another Abomination of Desolation that we have yet to uncover.

So I meticulously searched the Book of Daniel for this missing Abomination of Desolation. After some time, I discovered the Book of Daniel contained another Abomination of Desolation that I initially missed. Once I read this scripture, I immediately understood how I missed it. Notice what the Bible says in Daniel 9:27:

> "And he shall confirm the covenant

> with many for one week: and in the midst of the week he shall cause the sacrifice and the oblation to cease, and for the overspreading of abominations he shall make it desolate, even until the consummation, and that determined shall be poured upon the desolate."

Aha! Daniel *did* make another reference to the Abomination of Desolation, but I missed it because my initial search was specific to "abomination" (not abominations) or "desolation" (not desolate).

As I studied Daniel 9:27, I could see that this Abomination of Desolation was different from the other Abominations of Desolation in Daniel. This Abomination of Desolation referred to the Crucifixion of Christ. Notice, the first part of verse 27 says, *"And he shall confirm the covenant with many for one week: and in the midst of the week he shall cause the sacrifice and the oblation to cease..."* Jesus was the One who tried to confirm the covenant with the Jews but was crucified $3^{1/2}$ years into His ministry. The ceasing of the *sacrifice* and *oblation* is a reference to the effect that Christ's death had upon the sacrificial law. Colossians 2:14 confirms His death brought an end to these ordinances.

Then Daniel reveals that *"The overspreading of abominations he shall make it desolate."* This desolation refers to the destruction of Jerusalem. In case you are on the fence with this one point, all you need to do is read the verse that proceeds 27. Notice what it says:

> "And after threescore and two weeks shall Messiah be cut off, but not for himself: and the people of the prince that shall come shall destroy the city and the sanctuary; and the end thereof shall be with a flood, and unto the end of the war desolations are determined." Daniel 9:26

It should be clear to you as it was to me, that when Jesus said, "*The abomination of desolation, spoken of by Daniel the prophet*," he was referring to Daniel 9:26-27, not Daniel 8:13, not Daniel 11:31, and not Daniel 12:11.

I finally understood why Jesus wanted *whoso readeth* Daniel to understand what they were reading. Daniel contains two distinct Abominations of Desolation, but Jesus only referred to one Abomination of Desolation when He prophesied Jerusalem's destruction. This leaves us with one obvious question: What is the meaning of the other Abomination of Desolation spoken of by Daniel the prophet?

Chapter 3

A Second Abomination of Desolation

By now, I hope you can see that Daniel presented two different Abominations of Desolation. I also hope you understand Jesus' interpretation of the first Abomination referred to the actions of the Roman soldiers who surrounded Jerusalem prior to its destruction. When the meaning of the first Abomination became clear to me, I knew I wouldn't be satisfied until I understood the meaning of the second Abomination. So in order to understand this next Abomination, I attempted to use a resource that I often took advantage of when I was in college. This resource is called the internet!

Antiochus Epiphanes

I decided the internet would be a great starting point in order to help me understand the meaning of this second Abomination of Desolation. I opened an internet browser and began typing "Abomination" in its search box. The browser seemed to know what I was looking for as it added the remainder of the phrase to the search box. I quickly pressed the *enter* button on my keyboard, eager

Antiochus Epiphanes

to see what information would come back. I was not surprised to discover many of the search results connected the Abomination of Desolation to a king named Antiochus Epiphanes. I became familiar with Antiochus while writing my third book, *The Clear and Present Truth of the Daily Sacrifice*. If you read that book, you should be familiar with the Syrian ruler. However, if you are unfamiliar with the villainous king, Antiochus Epiphanes ruled Syria from 175 to 164 BC and is often designated as the individual responsible for the Abomination of Desolation. Here is what Rev. Joseph Benson wrote regarding Antiochus and the Abomination of Desolation:

> "We are informed by Josephus, by the author of the Maccabees, and others, that Antiochus's soldiers entered the temple and plundered it, and that afterward he ordered that the Jews should not be suffered to offer up the

daily sacrifices, which, according to the law, they were accustomed to offer; that he compelled them also to omit their worship of the true God, and to pay divine honours to them whom he regarded as gods, and to make shrines in every city and village, and to build altars, and daily to sacrifice swine upon them: see Joseph. Antiq. lib. 12. cap. 5, sec. 4. And they shall place the abomination that maketh desolate — In the Scriptures, idols are commonly called abominations. This was a prediction of the great profanation Antiochus should cause to the temple, in placing an idol upon the altar of burnt- offerings: see 1Ma 6:54; 1Ma 6:59. It is probable, that the idol was Jupiter, because we find that they dedicated the temple anew to Jupiter Olympus: see 2Ma 6:2. It is here called the abomination that maketh desolate, because it banished the true worship of God, and his worshippers, from the place."[8]

---

[8] Benson, Joseph. "Benson Commentary on the Old and New Testaments." Accessed September 22, 2020.
https://biblehub.com/commentaries/benson/daniel/11.htm

Mr. Benson is not alone in his thinking. In my research, I discovered there are a number of Bible scholars who believe Antiochus Epiphanes was the individual responsible for Daniel's Abomination of Desolation. And while I do believe this theology is erroneous, I can understand why Christians often invoke the Syrian king's name as the official villain of God's people. The fact that Antiochus attacked the Children of Israel and forced them into Pagan worship is definitely an abomination. And the fact that the king banished true worship from the sanctuary can be seen as a type of desolation. So yes, an argument can be made Antiochus Epiphanes' actions brought about an abomination that resulted in a desolation. But understand, even if we deduce this was an abomination of desolation, it still wasn't *THE* Abomination of Desolation in the Book of Daniel. How do we know this? As I studied the prophecies written in the Book of Daniel, I began to understand that the prophecies presented in Daniel 2, 7, 8, and 11-12 revolve around four kingdoms—Babylon, Medo-Persia, Greece, and Rome. Understand, these four kingdoms were not simultaneous world powers; their prominence came in succession. In other words, these four powers were never world powers at the same time; they each rose to prominence then fell as the succeeding kingdom became dominant.

Regarding this succession, Ellen White says,

"When Babylon fell, and Medo-Persia succeeded, it was overturned the first time. When Medo-Persia fell and was succeeded by Greece, it was overturned the second time. When the Greek empire gave way to Rome, it was overturned the third time. And then says the word, 'It shall be no more, until He come whose right it is; and I will give it Him.'" *Patriarchs and Prophets*, p. 762

Knowing the succession of these kingdoms helps us maintain prophetic integrity. What do I mean by the succession of kingdoms and prophetic integrity? Let me explain it like this: When I was younger, my mother gave me a coloring book and a box of crayons. When I began coloring in this book, I scribbled all over its pages with little regard for pictures and shapes. However, it wasn't long until I realized there were coloring rules. I discovered there was a reason images and shapes all had lines. These lines were there as borders, and in order to be a successful coloring book artist, I would have to color within these lines.

As simple as this concept is, we can apply this same principle to understanding Bible prophecy. Think of the four kingdoms as four different shapes in a coloring book.

| Babylon | Medo-Persia | Greece | Rome |

Each kingdom has its own set of lines or borders. If we want to be successful at interpreting Daniel's prophecies, we must first determine which kingdom was ruling at the time of the prophecy's fulfillment. Then we need to ensure our interpretation is consistent with the history of that kingdom. For example, if a prophecy pertains to the Babylonian Empire, there is no reason to look at events that happened during the reign of Persia as a fulfillment of that prophecy. If a prophecy occurred under Babylonian rule, then we must confine our interpretation of that prophecy to Babylonian history. This is what "coloring within the lines" means.

If prophecy determines Rome was in power when a prophecy was fulfilled, we cannot refer to events that occurred under Greek dominance as the fulfillment of that prophecy. We must stay within the lines! Now do you see why it's important to know the succession of kingdoms? Knowing the sequence that these kingdoms rose to power gives us our borders, and our borders give us our prophetic integrity.

By now, I'm sure you are wondering—How does knowing the succession of kingdoms or "coloring within the lines" relate to Antiochus Epiphanes? The answers to these questions will become clear once we establish which kingdom ruled the world at the time the Abomination of Desolation occurred. Pay close attention to what the prophet Daniel reveals in the following text:

> "After this I saw in the night visions, and behold a fourth beast, dreadful and terrible, and strong exceedingly; and it had great iron teeth: it devoured and brake in pieces, and stamped the residue with the feet of it: and it was diverse from all the beasts that were before it; and it had ten horns. I considered the horns, and, behold, there came up among them another little horn, before whom there were three of the first horns plucked up by the roots: and, behold, in this horn were eyes like the eyes of man, and a mouth speaking great things." Daniel 7:7-8

There are two things I need you to notice:

1) Daniel is referring to the Fourth Beast.
2) The Little Horn rose out of this Fourth Beast.

Now, according to the succession of kingdoms, which kingdom was the fourth world power?

If you answered "Rome," then you are correct; the fourth kingdom was Rome. So whenever we see the Little Horn, the Bible is referring to a component of the Roman Empire.

In the next chapter, Daniel expounds on this Little Horn of Rome. Notice how the prophet introduces this entity the second time:

> "And out of one of them came forth a little horn, which waxed exceeding great, toward the south, and toward the east, and toward the pleasant land." Daniel 8:9

Daniel continues telling us about this Little Horn. Notice what he reveals next:

> "And an host was given him against the daily sacrifice by reason of transgression, and it cast down the truth to the ground; and it practised, and prospered. Then I heard one saint speaking, and another saint said unto that certain saint which spake, How long shall be the vision concerning the daily sacrifice, and the transgression of desolation, to give both the sanctuary and the host to be trodden under foot?" Daniel 8:12-13

Notice, it was the Little Horn that was responsible for the Transgression of Desolation. This Transgression of Desolation is the same as the Abomination of Desolation found in Daniel 11 and 12. So here we have proof that a component of Rome was responsible for the Abomination of Desolation. But why is this a problem? It's a problem because Antiochus did not rise out of the Roman Empire! History tells us that when Alexander the Great died, his kingdom was divided.[9] Daniel 8:8 declares that out of that division, four main kings would rise. One in the north, one in the east, one in the south, and one in the west. After years of wars and conquests, Greece's four divisions became two divisions—north and south. Syria ruled the north, and Egypt ruled the south. Antiochus Epiphanes was simply one of the Syrian Kings who ruled the northern territory, but this was still under the divided Greek Empire. Antiochus rose out of Greece!

Now do you understand why it's important to "color" within the prophetic lines? The Little Horn, which was responsible for the Abomination of Desolation, came from Rome, not the divided Greek Empire.

Because we've determined Rome was the power responsible for the Abomination of Desolation, we cannot apply this prophecy's fulfillment to a Greek

---

[9] Wasson, Donald L. "Wars of the Diadochi." Ancient History Encyclopedia. Last modified July 14, 2016. https://www.ancient.eu/Wars_of_the_Diadochi/.

king. This eliminates Antiochus Epiphanes as the individual responsible for setting up the Abomination of Desolation; however, it doesn't reveal who was responsible.

I continued searching the internet and discovered another individual considered to be affiliated with the Abomination of Desolation. However, just as Evangelical books promoted Antiochus, this individual was promoted by a number of Seventh-day Adventist books. His name is Clovis.

Clovis I

Even though I had previously heard of Clovis's name, I never researched his life until I began studying the Abomination of Desolation. Upon learning that he may be significant to this book's focus, I decided to dedicate a substantial portion of my study time to learn more about him.

Knowing that the Abomination took place within

Clovis I of France

the dispensation of the Roman Empire, the first thing I needed to determine was if Clovis was within the "coloring lines" of Rome. I was relieved to discover that Clovis played a significant role in Roman history after

Western Rome fell to the invading tribes of the north. History says Clovis was the king of the Franks, a Germanic tribe that later became the country of France. What makes Clovis significant to prophecy is the fact that in 496 AD, he converted from Arian Christianity to Catholic Christianity.[10] According to a number of Adventist scholars, his conversion to Catholicism was the pivotal event that resulted in the Roman Empire's conversion to Catholicism. And because his conversion was pivotal for the conversion of the Empire, some believe his actions facilitated the establishment of the Abomination of Desolation. To buffer this point, I have quoted a few Adventist authors regarding Clovis and the Abomination of Desolation:

> "France, during the reign of Clovis, was the principal actor in placing 'the abomination.'" Apollos Hale, *The Second Advent Manual*, p. 83

> "William Miller (1782-1849), on his turn, believed (1) that both the 1,290 years and the 1,335 years had began in A.D. 508, with Clovis's victory over the Arian Visigoths, which was a decisive step in uniting both political

---

[10] Encyclopædia Britannica, s.v. "Clovis I," date accessed October 04, 2020, https://www.britannica.com/biography/Clovis-I.

and ecclesiastic powers for Medieval Catholicism to be able to punish the 'heretics'; (2) that the 1,290 years were fulfilled in 1798, with the imprisonment of Pope Pius VI by the French army; and (3) that the 1,335 years would extend for 45 years more, until the end of the 2300 years of Daniel 8:14 in 1843/1844.1[2] This interpretation was kept by early Sabbatarian Adventists,1 [3] becoming the historical position of the Seventh-day Adventist Church up to our own days." Alberto R. Timm, *The 1,290 and 1,335 Days of Daniel 12* [11]

How was the 'daily,' or paganism, taken away? As this is spoken of in connection with the placing or setting up of the abomination of desolation, or the papacy, it must denote, not merely the nominal change of the religion of the empire from paganism to Christianity, as on the so-called conversion of Constantine, but to such an

---

[11] Accessed October 18, 2020.
https://www.adventistbiblicalresearch.org/sites/default/files/pdf/daniel12_0.pdf

> eradication of paganism from all the elements of the empire that the way would be entirely open for the papal abomination to arise and assert its arrogant claims. Such a revolution as this was accomplished, but not for nearly two hundred years after the death of Constantine. As we approach the year AD 508, we behold a mighty crisis ripening between Catholicism and the pagan influences still existing in the empire. Up to the time of the conversion of Clovis, king of France, in AD 496, the French and other nations of Western Rome were pagan; but following that event, the efforts to convert idolaters to Romanism were crowned with great success. Uriah Smith, *Daniel and Revelation*, p. 272

From reading the above quotations, it appears some Adventist scholars believe the conversion of Clovis was the main factor that gave the Roman Catholic Church an edge over competing religious systems. Arianism and Paganism were competing for the region, but Catholicism would ultimately become the faith for the remaining Germanic tribes of the Roman Empire.

These Adventist scholars also endorse the idea that the Papacy was the Abomination of Desolation. They believe this Abomination was established as a result of Clovis's conversion to Catholicism, which by 508 AD influenced or forced the other tribes into the faith.

While I agree that Clovis was significant to the advancement of Catholicism in the Roman Empire, I believe a false perception of the Daily Sacrifice has prompted many of our Adventist scholars to mistakenly attribute the Abomination of Desolation to Clovis and the year 508 AD.

In my research, I discovered that many of our Adventist brethren believe the Daily Sacrifice was Paganism. Uriah Smith, in his book *The Daniel and Revelation*, attempts to explain this in the following manner:

> "It was shown in comments on Daniel 8: 13, that 'sacrifice' is a word erroneously supplied. It should be 'desolation.' The expression denotes a desolating power, of which the abomination of desolation is but the counterpart, and to which it succeeds in point of time. It seems clear therefore that the 'daily' desolation was paganism, and the 'abomination

of desolation' is the papacy." *Daniel and the Revelation* p. 271

It should be understood that Papal Rome did succeed Pagan Rome. The Bible says, "...*and the dragon* [Pagan Rome] *gave him* [Papal Rome] *his power, and his seat, and great authority.*" Revelation 13:2. It is this succession that has led many to believe the Daily Sacrifice was Paganism and the Abomination of Desolation was Catholicism. While this is a logical conclusion, I believe it is flawed. Regarding Papal Rome, Daniel 11:31 says, "...*and* [they] shall *take away the daily sacrifice.*" This taking away is not willingly; it is by force. However, Revelation 13 says the Dragon *gave* the Beast his power. This *giving* appears to be voluntary. Notice how Ellen White expresses this same idea:

> "The papacy received all its power from Satan." *The Great Controversy 1888*, p. 680

Some of us appear to be under the impression that the *taking away of the Daily* and the *giving away of the power, seat, and great authority* are the same historical event. However, we need to understand they are not the same. The transition of the Empire from Paganism to Catholicism was how the Dragon gave the Beast his power, seat, and great authority. However, once the Beast received that power, he then persecuted the saints! Please don't miss this! The power, seat, and great authority that the Dragon gave to the Beast, were the tools the Beast used to take away the Daily Sacrifice! The transition from Paganism to Catholicism is what enabled Catholicism to take away the Daily Sacrifice! This is why the Daily Sacrifice cannot be Paganism.

So now, the logical question is—What is the Daily Sacrifice? If you read my book *The Clear and Present Truth of The Daily Sacrifice*, you will understand that the Daily Sacrifice is the New Testament Church! The translators erroneously added the word *sacrifice* to the text, and the word *Daily* means "continual" in the original language. In essence, the Christian Church is the CONTINUATION of Israel. And it was the Christian Church that was taken away in the sixth century and replaced by the Abomination of Desolation, or what we call the Papacy. Notice how Ellen White expresses this idea:

> "In the sixth century the Papacy had become firmly established. Its seat of power was fixed in the imperial city, and the Bishop of Rome was declared to be the head over the entire church. Paganism had given place to the Papacy. The dragon had given to the beast '*his power, and his seat, and great authority.*' Revelation 13:2. And now began the 1260 years of papal

oppression foretold in the prophecies of Daniel and John. (Daniel 7:25; Revelation 13:5-7.) Christians were forced to choose, either to yield their integrity and accept the papal ceremonies and worship, or to wear away their lives in dungeon cells, or suffer death by the rack, the fagot, or the headsman's ax. Now were fulfilled the words of Jesus, 'Ye shall be betrayed both by parents, and brethren, and kinsfolks, and friends; and some of you shall they cause to be put to death. And ye shall be hated of all men for My name's sake.'" *The Story of Redemption*, p. 330

Paganism, through Satan, willingly gave the Papacy its power. The Papacy used that power to take away the Daily (pure Christianity) by force and set up the Abomination of Desolation. Remember, the Abomination of Desolation is the infiltration of Paganism into God's territory, not the infiltration of Paganism into Pagan territory.[12] Think about it this way: the conversion of the Western Roman Empire to Catholicism would mean very little to Satan if true Christians did not compromise their faith. From its

---

[12] Paganism and Satanic forces are used interchangeably.

inception, Rome was Pagan, but that was never considered the Abomination of Desolation because God's people did not compromise and convert. It wasn't until Paganism was "baptized" and repackaged in the form of Catholicism that prophecy foresaw an Abomination on the horizon.

An Abomination occurs when good is mixed with evil, when truth is mixed with error, or when holy is mixed with secular. This *mixture,* which causes ruin or Desolation, is found throughout the Bible even though the scriptures may not use the Abomination of Desolation phrase. Here are a few examples:

> "Woe unto them that call evil good, and good evil; that put darkness for light, and light for darkness; that put bitter for sweet, and sweet for bitter!" Isaiah 5:20

> "Know ye not that ye are the temple of God, and that the Spirit of God dwelleth in you? If any man defile the temple of God, him shall God destroy; for the temple of God is holy, which temple ye are." 1Corinthians 3:16-17

> "Judah hath dealt treacherously, and an abomination is committed in Israel and in Jerusalem; for Judah

> hath profaned the holiness of the LORD which he loved, and hath married the daughter of a strange god. The LORD will cut off the man that doeth this..." Malachi 2:11-12.

The *mixture* is the Abomination, not the expansion of that mixture. The Franks expanded Catholicism among the Arian and Pagan tribes, but they were not the reason for the mass deception among God's people. Clovis may be viewed as an extension of the Papal power, but he was not the mastermind behind the Great Apostasy of the Church. In other words, Clovis *enforced* Catholicism, but he was not the reason for true Christianity's *acceptance* of Catholicism. Well, if Clovis was not responsible for the establishment of the Abomination, then who was? The answer is the Bishop of Rome.

The Bishop of Rome

The Bishop of Rome is the power that was responsible for the Great Apostasy among God's people. Ellen White confirms this viewpoint with the following statement:

> "To secure worldly gains and honors, the church was led to seek the favor and support of the great men of earth, and having thus rejected Christ, she

> was induced to yield allegiance to the representative of Satan,—the bishop of Rome." *The Great Controversy 1888*, p. 50

Here, the Bishop of Rome is not a particular individual. He represents the system that took away true Christianity and replaced it with an apostate form of religion. The Bishop of Rome is the same entity that scripture calls the Little Horn. If there's any confusion about who the Little Horn is, I hope this statement from Ellen White brings clarity to the subject:

> "The prophet Daniel declared that the Roman Church, symbolized by the little horn, was to think to change times and laws..." *The Great Controversy 1888*, p. 446

According to Ellen White, the Little Horn represents the Roman Church, not King Clovis I. And while some still believe Clovis took away the Daily Sacrifice, there is no doubt in my mind that the same entity who took away the Daily Sacrifice was the same entity that set up the Abomination of Desolation. The entity was the Bishop of Rome, which is also synonymous with Catholicism, the Roman Church, and the Papacy.

Daniel 7:25 tells us the steps the Papacy took in

order to take pure Christianity away. The prophet says the Papacy will "*speak great words against the most High, and shall wear out the saints of the most High, and think to change times and laws.*" This is how the Christian Church was nearly annihilated during the Dark Ages. The Papacy's great words deceived the saints into believing the church was above the Bible. The wearing-out or persecution of the saints made the true church go into hiding. Finally, the changing of times (Sabbath to Sunday) and laws (commandment regarding image worship) enabled the replacement of the Daily with the Abomination of Desolation.

John the Revelator also identified the Daily (true religion) and the Abomination of Desolation (false religion). Notice how God revealed both churches to him:

> "And there appeared a great wonder in heaven; a woman clothed with the sun, and the moon under her feet, and upon her head a crown of twelve stars." Revelation 12:1

In Bible prophecy, a woman is often used to symbolize God's people.[13] This pure woman, clothed with the sun, moon, and stars, represents the true church, which is also the Daily (continuation) of Israel.

---

[13] 2Corinthians 11:2

However, there would come a time when the true church would almost be eradicated, and a false church would take her place. Notice how John describes this new woman:

> "So he carried me away in the spirit into the wilderness: and I saw a woman sit upon a scarlet coloured beast, full of names of blasphemy, having seven heads and ten horns. And the woman was arrayed in purple and scarlet colour, and decked with gold and precious stones and pearls, having a golden cup in her hand full of abominations and filthiness of her fornication: And upon her forehead was a name written, MYSTERY, BABYLON THE GREAT, THE MOTHER OF HARLOTS AND ABOMINATIONS OF THE EARTH." Revelation 17:4-5

The first woman represents the Daily, and the second woman represents the Abomination of Desolation. Notice how Ellen White described the transition from the Daily to the Abomination of Desolation:

> "The accession of the Roman Church

to power marked the beginning of the Dark Ages. As her power increased, the darkness deepened. Faith was transferred from Christ, the true foundation, to the pope of Rome. Instead of trusting in the Son of God for forgiveness of sins and for eternal salvation, the people looked to the pope, and to the priests and prelates to whom he delegated authority. They were taught that the pope was their earthly mediator, and that none could approach God except through him, and, further, that he stood in the place of God to them, and was therefore to be implicitly obeyed. A deviation from his requirements was sufficient cause for the severest punishment to be visited upon the bodies and souls of the offenders. Thus the minds of the people were turned away from God to fallible, erring, and cruel men, nay more, to the prince of darkness himself, who exercised his power through them. Sin was disguised in a garb of sanctity. When the Scriptures are suppressed, and man comes to regard

> himself as supreme, we need look only for fraud, deception, and debasing iniquity. With the elevation of human laws and traditions, was manifest the corruption that ever results from setting aside the law of God." *The Great Controversy 1888*, p. 55

Once the Little Horn "*cast down the truth to the ground*,"[14] he was able to set up the Abomination of Desolation. At that point, the saints were "*given into his [the Little Horn's] hand until a time and times and the dividing of time.*"[15] Regarding this period, Ellen White says the following:

> "The forty and two months are the same as the "time and times and the dividing of time," three years and a half, or 1260 days, of Daniel 7 - - the time during which the papal power was to oppress God's people. This period, as stated in preceding chapters, began with the supremacy of the papacy, A.D. 538, and

---

[14] Daniel 8:12
[15] Daniel 7:25

terminated in 1798." *The Great Controversy*, p. 439

By now, I hope you understand that the Little Horn (the Bishop of Rome) was the entity the prophet Daniel referred to when he spoke about the Abomination of Desolation. I also hope you understand that there are two Abominations of Desolation mentioned in scripture:

> 1). In 70 AD, Pagan Roman soldiers infiltrated the holy grounds of Jerusalem before destroying it. This was the first Abomination of Desolation.
>
> 2). In 538 AD, Pagan doctrines infiltrated the holy grounds of the church, giving precedence to an amalgamation of Paganism and Christianity. This was the second Abomination, which brought Desolation to the church for 1260 years.

Now do you understand why it's important to have a proper understanding of the Abomination of Desolation? Having a proper understanding of this doctrine may not determine your salvation, but it will definitely give you a clearer understanding of Daniel's prophecies. Daniel specified two Abominations of Desolation; however, would you believe me if I told you there is still more to uncover? You see, I was under the impression that the Abomination of Desolation only pertained to past events; however, as I continued to study, I realized that the Abomination of Desolation is also a future event! Ladies and Gentlemen, a third Abomination of Desolation is coming!

Chapter 4

A Third Abomination of Desolation

In my book, *The Clear and Present Truth of 666*, you will discover that the Dragon, Beast, and False Prophet[16] represent three phases of the same persecuting power. The Dragon represents Pagan Rome, the Beast represents Papal Rome, and the False Prophet represents Protestant America. If you're wondering how these three powers relate to the Abomination of Desolation, then allow me to point out that Pagan Rome established the first Abomination and Papal Rome established the second.

Now here is where it gets interesting. Would you believe me if I told you there was a third Abomination of Desolation? The good thing is, you don't have to believe me.

Notice how Ellen White describes Satan's end-time strategy against God's people:

---

[16] Revelation 16:13

> "One effort more, and then Satan's last device is employed. He hears the unceasing cry for Christ to come, for Christ to deliver them. This last strategy is to personate Christ and make them think their prayers are answered. But this answers to the last closing work, the abomination of desolation standing in the holy place." *Manuscript 16, 1884*

Do you see this? Ellen White has thrown off our prophetic equilibrium by declaring a third Abomination of Desolation! She doesn't mince words. She plainly tells us Satan's personation of Christ is another Abomination of Desolation. However, before we move any further, we must validate Ellen White's statement from the Bible. If Ellen White claims Satan will appear as Jesus, we should be able to find this principle in the Word of God.

In reading the New Testament, you will discover this principle is found in the writings of Paul. In his second letter to the Corinthians, Paul reveals to us that Satan will masquerade himself as an angel of light. Notice how scripture conveys this deception:

> "And no marvel; for Satan himself is transformed into an angel of light." 2Corinthians 11:14

So, according to Paul, Satan will masquerade himself as an angel of light. Here, I believe we should ask ourselves this question—Why would Satan, who is considered the chief *ruler of the darkness of this world*,[17] transform himself into an angel of light? The answer was given to us by Jesus Christ himself:

> "For there shall arise false Christs, and false prophets, and shall shew great signs and wonders; insomuch that, if it were possible, they shall deceive the very elect." Matthew 24:24

Satan's angelic transformation is designed for one purpose: to deceive the world into giving him what he's always desired—worship. Satan has always wanted to be worshiped, and he knows the only way to receive this worship is for the world to believe he is God. Therefore, Satan will display great signs and wonders, and one of these wonders will be the transformation of himself into a false Christ. This Satanic transformation is what Ellen White calls *the last closing work* and an *Abomination of Desolation*.

Remember, the Abomination of Desolation is the infiltration of Satanic forces into God's territory. I admit, this definition made it hard for me to

---

[17] Ephesians 6:12

understand how Satan's personation of Christ could be considered an Abomination of Desolation. But then the thought occurred to me—If Satan pretends he is Christ, and Christians worship him, then this is still a Satanic infiltration into God's territory.

If you recall, during the first two Abominations, Satan used Pagans to infiltrate God's territory. However, for this final deception, Satan will not outsource the Abomination to a third-party. "*Satan himself*" will perform this Abomination of Desolation!

Now that we understand what the third Abomination is and who establishes it, we can better determine which nation will be the presiding world power during its manifestation. John introduces this end-time world power with these words:

> "And I beheld another beast coming up out of the earth; and he had two horns like a lamb, and he spake as a dragon." Revelation 13:11

Bible prophecy typically uses beasts to symbolize nations.[18] After studying the characteristics of this Lamblike creature, I concluded that this Beast represented the United States of America.[19] Ellen White's commentary on Revelation 13 also makes this

---

[18] See Daniel 7:23
[19] Details of this study are documented in The Clear and Present Truth of 666.

same declaration:

> "It has been shown that the United States is the power represented by the beast with lamblike horns..." *The Great Controversy*, p. 578

According to Revelation 13, this Lamblike Beast will be the leading nation used by Satan to deceive the world. John the Revelator says,

> "And he doeth great wonders, so that he maketh fire come down from heaven on the earth in the sight of men, And deceiveth them that dwell on the earth by the means of those miracles which he had power to do in the sight of the beast..." Revelation 13:13-14

From these scriptures, we can deduce that America will be aided by wonders and miracles in order to deceive the world. However, from Ellen White's commentary, we can understand Satan's personation of Christ is part of the wonders and miracles performed through the Lamblike Beast.

> "He ... deceiveth them that dwell on the earth by the means of those miracles which he had power to do,"

> not merely those which he pretends to do. Something more than mere impostures is brought to view in this scripture. But there is a limit beyond which Satan cannot go, and here he calls deception to his aid and counterfeits the work which he has not power actually to perform. In the last days he will appear in such a manner as to make men believe him to be Christ come the second time into the world. He will indeed transform himself into an angel of light." Ellen White *Testimonies for the Church*, vol. 5, p. 698

Now it makes sense why Jesus said, "*Every kingdom divided against itself is brought to desolation; and every city or house divided against itself shall not stand.*"[20] The Abomination is a spiritual conflict of interest. The result of this conflict is Desolation.

There is a final Abomination coming. We must understand this final Abomination leads to a final Desolation—which is the destruction of the wicked and the earth.

The Bible paints a picture of this Desolation,

---
[20] Matthew 12:24

which commences with the seven last plagues and culminates at the Second Coming of Christ:

> "Behold, the LORD maketh the earth empty, and maketh it waste, and turneth it upside down, and scattereth abroad the inhabitants thereof." Isaiah 24:1

> "I beheld the earth, and, lo, it was without form, and void; and the heavens, and they had no light. I beheld the mountains, and, lo, they trembled, and all the hills moved lightly. I beheld, and, lo, there was no man, and all the birds of the heavens were fled. I beheld, and, lo, the fruitful place was a wilderness, and all the cities thereof were broken down at the presence of the LORD, and by his fierce anger. For thus hath the LORD said, The whole land shall be desolate; yet will I not make a full end." Jeremiah 4:23-27

> "And the slain of the LORD shall be at that day from one end of the earth even unto the other end of the earth: they shall not be lamented, neither

> gathered, nor buried; they shall be dung upon the ground." Jeremiah 25:33

> "And ye shall tread down the wicked; for they shall be ashes under the soles of your feet in the day that I shall do this, saith the LORD of hosts." Malachi 4:3

Satan is the one who sets up the final Abomination; however, God is the One who will execute the final Desolation; and the results of this Desolation are eternal.

Remember, the Abomination of Desolation is always the infiltration of Satanic forces into God's territory. Understanding this, we should know that two Abominations of Desolation have already occurred, and a third Abomination is soon to come. The first was issued by the Dragon, the second was issued by the Beast, and the third will be established through the False Prophet.

Some of us may believe the Abomination of Desolation only affects us from a church or collective standpoint, but I implore you to also think of it from an individual perspective. This requires all of us to ask the question—Am I allowing an Abomination of Desolation in my personal life? If God is the true ruler of our lives, then everything we own is part of His territory.

However, when we allow Satan into territory designated for God, we establish individual Abominations of Desolation that stand in places that should be holy. Our cars, homes, marriages, and even our minds should be holy grounds. However, if we find ourselves compromising with Satan, then that's an indication we have set up an individual Abomination of Desolation. Allowing these personal Abominations into our lives prepares us to accept the third and final Abomination of Desolation.

  Time is short! The first two Abominations of Desolation have passed, but that doesn't mean we should let our guards down. Now is the time for us to pray and fortify our minds with the Word of God. A final Abomination of Desolation is on the horizon, and many of God's people will not be ready for it. This message needs to be taught to the world, which is why you are reading this book. I truly believe God placed you here for such a time as this. We have a lot of work to do, with little time to do it. People may reject this book's message, but this should not stop us from giving them *The Clear and Present Truth of the Abomination of Desolation*.

THE CLEAR AND PRESENT TRUTH OF THE
ABOMINATION OF DESOLATION

TEST YOUR KNOWLEDGE

1. Matthew 24 is a two-fold prophecy that reveals the destruction of the world and the destruction of what city? (p. 11)

   _____

2. According to Luke, what historical event fulfilled the specific Abomination of Desolation referred to by Jesus? (pp. 16-17)

   _____
   _____
   _____

3. The Abomination of Desolation will always mean this. (p. 20)

   _____
   _____
   _____

4. Not one _____ perished in the destruction of Jerusalem. (p. 18)

5. The prophet Daniel refers to the Transgression/ Abomination of Desolation four times. List all four scripture references. (pp. 24-25, 30-31)

   _____
   _____

6. Jesus talked about the Abomination of Desolation, spoken of by Daniel the prophet. Of the four references Daniel made to the Abomination of Desolation, which one was Jesus alluding to in Matthew 24:15? (p. 32)

7. Explain why Antiochus Epiphanes was not the individual who set up the Abomination of Desolation. (pp. 41-42)

8. Explain why Clovis was not the individual that set up the Abomination of Desolation. (pp. 46-52)

9. What does the Daily Sacrifice represent? (p. 48)

10. How did the Little Horn take away the Daily? (pp. 52-53)

11. Describe the first two Abominations of Desolation. (pp. 57)

12. Explain the third Abomination of Desolation. (pp. 60-61)

Test Your Knowledge • 73

ANSWERS

1. Matthew 24 is a two-fold prophecy that reveals the destruction of the world and the destruction of what city?
   Jerusalem

2. According to Luke, what historical event fulfilled the specific Abomination of Desolation referred to by Jesus? **When Jerusalem was compassed with armies and later destroyed.**

3. The Abomination of Desolation will always mean this: **The Abomination of Desolation occurs when God's territory is invaded by Satanic forces, which eventually brings ruin to God's people.**

4. Not one **Christian** perished in the destruction of Jerusalem.

5. The prophet Daniel refers to the Transgression/ Abomination of Desolation four times. List all four scripture references. **Daniel 8:13, Daniel 11:31, Daniel 12:11, and Daniel 9:27**

6. Jesus talked about the Abomination of Desolation, spoken of by Daniel the prophet. Of the four references Daniel made to the Abomination of Desolation, which one was Jesus alluding to in Matthew 24:15? **Daniel 9:27**

7. Explain why Antiochus Epiphanes was not the individual who set up the Abomination of Desolation. **The Little Horn was responsible for taking away the Daily and the setting up of the Abomination of Desolation. The Little Horn came out of the Roman Empire; however, Antiochus rose up out of the divided Greek Empire.**

TEST YOUR KNOWLEDGE • 75

8. Explain why Clovis I was not the individual that set up the Abomination of Desolation. **a). Clovis was the enforcer for the Catholic Church, but he was not the mastermind behind the Great apostasy of the church. b). The Little Horn set up the Abomination of Desolation, not Clovis. c). Ellen White confirms The Little Horn is not Clovis; the Little Horn is the Papacy.**

9. What does the Daily Sacrifice represent? **The Church**

10. How did the Little Horn take away the Daily?
    - **Making the church believe it was above the Bible**
    - **Persecution of the saints**
    - **Making it appear that the law of God had changed**

11. Describe the first two Abominations of Desolation.
- **In 70 AD, Pagan Roman soldiers infiltrated the holy grounds of Jerusalem before destroying it. This was the first Abomination of Desolation.**
- **In 538 AD, Pagan doctrines infiltrated the holy grounds of the church, giving precedence to an amalgamation of Paganism and Christianity. This was the second Abomination, which brought Desolation to the church for 1260 years.**

12. Explain the third Abomination of Desolation. **Satan personating Christ and deceiving believers into worshipping him. This will lead the deceived to the desolation of hellfire.**

www.ingramcontent.com/pod-product-compliance
Lightning Source LLC
Chambersburg PA
CBHW062150100526
44589CB00014B/1775